INTENTION OF THE WORD

Edited by

Chiara Cervasio

First published in Great Britain in 2004 by
POETRY NOW
Remus House,
Coltsfoot Drive,
Peterborough, PE2 9JX
Telephone (01733) 898101
Fax (01733) 313524

SB ISBN 1 84460 815 8

FOREWORD

Although we are a nation of poets we are accused of not reading poetry, or buying poetry books. After many years of listening to the incessant gripes of poetry publishers, I can only assume that the books they publish, in general, are books that most people do not want to read.

Poetry should not be obscure, introverted, and as cryptic as a crossword puzzle: it is the poet's duty to reach out and embrace the world.

The world owes the poet nothing and we should not be expected to dig and delve into a rambling discourse searching for some inner meaning.

The reason we write poetry (and almost all of us do) is because we want to communicate: an ideal; an idea; or a specific feeling. Poetry is as essential in communication, as a letter; a radio; a telephone, and the main criterion for selecting the poems in this anthology is very simple: they communicate.

CONTENTS

THE DAY WE TALKED WITH AN ARAN-ISLANDER

Together in Conamara with the bleak and beautiful
Queen Maeve of Connaught on our shoulders
The Carolan Concerto upon the hills
I had my father to myself for part of a priceless day,
We talked of things from dream time
What the sky looks like and the stars that we are,
Until we reached the west coast, drew breath to view
Upon scenes of exceptional green and blue.
We looked at the islands
And he told me about those people who were so special
On a different level,
Nearby . . .
There was an old white thatch-roofed building on a rocky outcrop
Looked so precarious but you felt it should be there
And we went in.
It was ancient with reliquary
Tears of joy still hit me in this reverie . . .
There, an old and friendly man greeted us
His sharp chiselled features
With the toothy grin
Cloth cap and rough-hewn ash cane,
Treated us to whiskey
And my father thanked him in Gaelic.
They were as one and I was a watcher
And although I could not understand the words, I knew the muse
And I could see their spirits dancing
My thoughts were free
Now I think of Turlough O'Carolan, 'the last of the bards',
But it was different then, I was innocent, pure
With an old man who showed us a bridge to the sky
Mine and yours to use to rise
And vanish in the clouds.

Patrick Brett

THE CRUCIFIXES

At the cross

I can taste the terrible trauma
And crucifixion of the death,

I can smell the sadness and the
Pain of Jesus' friends.

I can see the terror of Jesus'
Mother and her crying eyes.

I can hear the cry and agony
Of Jesus' mother and the
Cheerful laughter of soldiers.

And in my heart I feel
That Jesus should be alive.

I can touch the rough cross
Jesus is nailed onto at his death.

Hayley Carr

ONE OF THE PACK

On centre stage of worldly hopes she laughs
Like a nightmare as rows of grinning teeth
Are ready to tear the remnants for their ration
Of acceptable emaciation from this creature
Robbed of flesh by the vagaries of fashion.

Sharp claws are honed to kill, for beauty is a
Painted mask filling hollow, brittle bones.
She-animal in fake fur stalks the narrow ridge
Of wealth with respectable starvation
This soulmate of her vanity reflects her inner self.

Pulsating rhythm, hot-arc lights scorching
Slippery earth, strive to be noticed, strive to provide,
She needs to be cunning, needs to connive
If she is to survive.

The pack are cold as winter light, only the
Strong will live on to fight. Her cubs are
Weak through world of plenty, fragile as
The ecosphere surrounding their world of fact.

Delyse Holmes

WHAT DO YOU SEE?

What do you see
When you look at me?
Do you see my spirituality,
Do you see my sensuality,
Or do you see just me?
Do you recognise I have a spirit
Living within me?
Do you recognise without this spirit I could not be,
Without this spirit there would be no me?
So I ask again
What do you see
When you look at me?

Yvette De Cordova

LEAVING SCHOOL

I will always remember perfect PE
Art for ace and moving music.

I always didn't get horrible history,
Silly science and mega maths.

I was neat on loony literacy,
Racing reading and sweet swimming.

Too hard to do the reality RE
Silly sports and performance of plays.

I didn't do beauty bikes,
Freaky French or Jerky German.

I will sadly miss torturing teachers,
Cheesy children and cosy classroom.

Perry Flowers (11)

A POISONING ON THE QUIET

But what is God? That's the focus
See within the folds, take some notice,
Given what is written,
Bite the chord and walk away.
It's bigger things which oversee,
As little s***s pass wind with glee,
Holding up staple diets,
A poisoning on the quiet.
If sin is the ticket that takes you there,
Go for a spin and let down your hair,
Don't turn your back from invention,
Progress is the intention.
What good is a could,
When only a can will do?

C T W P Darkly

DADDY

Daddy, do not go.
Mummy's crying tears,
Your little boy needs you
In his tender years.
Daddy, do not go.
Who would tuck me in
At bedtime? I just need you,
Just as it's always been.
Daddy, do not go.
Mummy's crying tears,
She said she still loves you,
Please take away her fears.
Your daughter is fast asleep,
She doesn't understand,
She's too young to weep
Or even hold your hand.
Daddy I just need you
To love me like you do,
Please do not go away,
Mummy needs you too.

E J Bishop

FOREVER

I wish I could see into your thoughts and read your mind,
Answer your prayers and wishes from within and make your
heart smile
When you lose somebody special nothing prepares you for that day,
Only God above can help that pain go away.
Remember the memories and special times that you shared,
Even if you laugh or smile instead of frown or cry
It doesn't mean to say you don't care.
Your husband, father, grandad, someone special has gone away
But is forever here in your thoughts and heart.
Only you know how you're feeling, only you know when to start
Understanding love, appreciation, admiration and adoration
Of our beloved ones when they sadly part.
May your grandad rest in peace and live forever in your heart.

C T Drepaul

THE PRISONER

Every day for him is the same
For he knows that he is to blame
If only he had stayed in that night
And not gone out and chose to fight
The lawyers did not work too hard
In fact, he thinks they should be barred
He went to court and lost the case
They saw the look upon his face

If only he could hold his beer
He would still be out
He would still be here
If only he had stayed at home that night
If only he could put things right
Breathing in the acrid smell
This must be it
This must be Hell

He made mistakes and got involved
In problems that were not his to solve
So now he sits
He has time to think
If only I had not had that drink
Night has come but still no rest
As roaches emerge from their nest
Night has come and still no sleep

Around his cell he starts to creep
Thinking, *I can't take no more*
He's out of it, he's on the floor
And these words ring within in his ears
'You're going down, you have got four years'

Raven Thunder

THE HERALD

It is 3am on a wet night.
Bleary street lamps guide the sonorous spinning wheels as
muddied droplets shimmer and hiss at their indecent haste.
Blue beams, gentle, hypnotic, bear down upon their sanctuary.
The engine labours. Too much time, too little speed.
A breeze whispers encouragement, fretful, expectant.
Wheels now stand idle like restless horses pawing at the ground.
Droplets form on smooth-transparent brows to be wiped away
by trance-like fingers. Silence but for the beat of the rain.
But now a shout! Forward! Urgent!
Gears grind, the engine throbs. A siren shatters the calm of
waiting. Wheels scramble to grasp at nettles on the softened
verges. Puddles jump up and join in the excitement.

The tall glass tower stands ready, newly washed with needles
of rain. A rinse of blue softens its harsh, sterile lines.
As the engine dies the siren stops and listens.
A gulp of air
a tentative whimper
magical.

Hands shake, smiles tremor, tears flow in tender acquiescence.
Each one different, every one a miracle.
Take five
relax and watch the rain.

Two hours have passed as blue beams dance along a road that
loops and twists like gleaming black ribbon, the keening of the
siren alerts the shocked and silent group. Fresh eyes take in the
horror, the carnage, the mortal sin of excess.
The relentless rain raps out an eerie tattoo on the scarred and
tortured metal. A macabre sculpture lays forlorn and lifeless; a
creature beaten into exhausted submission.
Flashing bulbs of blue rotate, obscene in their brightness
ghoulish spectators around a silent arena.

Radios spew out distorted voices, intrusive, unmoved, efficient.
Fluorescent figures seemingly disorganised gesture and point,
their shouts become urgent, triumphant. Machines vibrate,
blades whine as if their summoning is long overdue. Sparks
momentarily illuminate faces, watchful, expectant. Gentle hands
pluck the battered scapegoats from their self-made mantrap.
They are borne away from their sodden shroud of darkness.

Water gurgles along the muddied verges glistening, unrepentant.
A house crouched by the roadside stares unblinking, its
rain-lashed face immovable, unreadable as the blue flashes by.
The audience participation over, the crowd disperses. Two are
left to walk in measured steps retracing, re-enacting, unaware
the house, their only witness, watches them in misery
and mute despair.

Vivien Exall

BRIEF ENCOUNTERS

As the train slowly pulls out clicking its carriages as passing seconds
To somewhere leaving the light, where it's been,
And you listen to its half-grasping, clicking words of wisdom
If you could pull that Excalibur back for just one moment . . .
As it evaporates into its yellow fog
You would be a king; for that moment, forever.

T L James

FISTS

No matter how many times I've said it before,
I guess I'm just gonna havta say it all the more:
I'm not f***ing living in fear of your fists,
Driving me insane with your paranoid fits,
If it happens once more I'll be out that door,
This ain't no relationship, feels more like a chore.
I know it's not your fault; it's the way you were brought up,
But man start to realise you cause your own f**k-ups.
You say it's my fault, I make you angry,
Can't you see I'm begging? Stop blaming me.
You pinned me down, your hand gripping my neck,
Look in my eyes and see that you left me a wreck.
I've never been scared of just one person up until you,
This relationship's over, ain't nothing you can do.
You're no longer the person you used to be,
I look at you now, and it's not you I see,
You're no longer the person I fell in love with,
I need some give and take, not you take and I give.
Maybe I'm just the one that sparks off your temper,
Pain caused, bruises left, your love I try to remember.
These days when the words 'I love you' leave your lips,
I don't look into your eyes anymore; I look down at your fists.

Sarah Sproston

THE GREYHOUND

I met Alf in a local club,
He was sitting drinking orange juice,
A quiet man with a good heart,
You know the sort.
I sat by him playing bingo,
When I thought to ask about his dog,
A greyhound.
I'd heard about it breaking its back,
Racing too hard as sometimes happens.
But Alf, undeterred
Told me this was true.
And as the numbers were called;
Boxes crossed;
Orange juice sipped,
He continued to say that
Although the vet had
Wanted to put the dog down,
He had insisted on nursing him,
Because he'd more than earned his keep.
And one day, some weeks later, the dog
Began to yelp, so Alf, who'd been carrying him,
Set him on his feet and the dog walked!
'That were four year' since,'
He said proudly.
Alf thinks the same could work for humans,
If they're loved and carried about for a while.

Janet M Kimmons

BLEW IT

Jeans aren't really jeans without it,
Boys go mad for it,
Especially those movies.
Pumping through the aristocracy,
Its music is mainly black!
A master plan for building
Buildings, buildings, buildings
It's handy in an emergency
And supports the Tories!
From nowhere it paints the skies,
At uni it plays for the team,
Leading the field in high finance
Even though the collars do the graft,
Colouring the air with language
When hammers blood-blister thumbs.
It wins all of the prizes
Yet its bells don't ring out in triumph,
Waltzing down the Danube,
Sand-dancing up Nile,
Cementing its reputation
Having a whale of a time.
All the world knows
It strikes a line through sensitive material
And how depressing it can be,
So even educated girls can succumb
To its illicit temptation;
Then when the terror becomes overbearing
They dig in to escape
And kneel there for three days
Frozen, cold-veined marble statues,
Waiting for the blowfly eggs to hatch,
Crumbling like unfridged Danish cheese.

Derek Kempthorne

THE MIGHTY STORM

On one of the stormiest nights,
Thunder rumbled like the roar of a dragon,
Lightning flashed like the blink of an eye,
Tornados blew like a charging rhino,
Whirlpools spun like a rolling armadillo,
Volcanoes erupted like a tempered bull.
Stampedes shook the earth
And rain flooded the world.

Sammy Alom (12)

NOWHERE

To go nowhere is to go where?
Where do we come from,
Do we just come and go, and say nothing,
Or do we just go nowhere?
I look and stare, I hope and pray, but for what?
The light is on, the light is off (who cares?),
Love, what is love, to love, or to be loved?
Love is to care and to be cared for,
So when you go to find and find what you want,
Is like going nowhere, to go where?

Confused? Join the club.

T Thwaites

MY BELOVED ENGLAND

I'd wandered far from home and friends
And stayed long, in a foreign land;
But like a magnet, I was drawn
Back to my country, England.

The journey on the boat was long,
Tired was this old sea rover.
Then came a precious sight indeed,
The grand white cliffs of Dover

The years fell from me like a robe,
Gone was regret for 'might-have-beens'
As, bright of eye, I gazed anew,
On half-forgotten childhood scenes.

Each blade of grass seemed twice as green,
The sky above more bright and blue.
My yearning heart knew peace at last,
Hope filled my breast with joy anew.

Since then, old age has touched my brow,
Silvery-white my hair has grown;
But in this wooded valley green,
Such blessed happiness I've known.

Time passes, like an ebbing tide,
My last farewell is close at hand.
Gladly I'll rest in yonder mound,
In my beloved England.

Rose Sutton

I'M DROWNING

I'm drowning in my life, please help me someone, please,
I'm losing what little I had and I'm falling to my knees,
The trust I had is slowly waning, even I am sick of my complaining,
But no one listens to what I feel, and now my head it starts to reel,
I've done my best these past few years, and have tried to hide my
pain and tears,
It's not enough I now realise; no one is listening to my cries,
I feel I've failed in every respect, even those I have tried to protect,
I needed to sort my inner pain, before I could begin again,
Now it's too late, what can I do? My big mistake as loving you.
I'm tired now, I need to sleep, it's perhaps too late to think so deep,
But some things are better written down and in the morning I'll
look and frown

Life's tough, I know that well; what's in store, who can tell?
Just give me a break!

Ann Robinson

THE TEMPERATE ZONE

A promissory note from weathergirls
who foretold it would be *nice*
and so it was and is and shall be.

But I'm bored with this and I want *weather,*
nothing temperate, but of extremes,
so even heatwaves seem exciting.

I demand an unexpected thunderstorm
with aerials torn and gutters bulging,
streetlights creeping on at noon;

Order the fall of housed barometers,
fist-sized hail ending a sudden game
and not a day for moderation.

A blizzard would be good. A racing front,
a wall of snow whipped by hysterical gales,
a storm we can take comfort from, indoors.

Not this 'have-a-nice-day' weather,
an average day this time of year.
It's lovely out, and calm – I want mad skies.

Bruce McRae

TIME

What is time?
The hands on a clock timing every second of every minute,
Every minute of every hour, every hour of every day?
Or is time defined as sunset and sunrise?
For many, time is a restriction on life,
And the words don't have time.
If people would stop and embrace life
And the time we have on this world
To stop and open their eyes to see,
Birds, trees, people walking down the street,
But many rely on time to finish work, to go out with friends,
Where would we be without time?
Nothing would get done.
Is time a gift to ensure order, to open your life?
For after life the there is only death.

Joanne Armstrong (17)

PAPA

His tanned face
An eggshell mosaic.
Time has dragged
The plough of experience
Over swarthy skin.
Ruts and ravines
Testify to struggles
Bravely borne.
His furrowed forehead
An atlas of life.
A mercury thatch
Of haphazard hair
Clings to a freckled dome.
Large hands,
Rough with calluses
Capable of cruelty,
Yet never raised in anger.
Ragged nails,
Constantly contaminated
By oozing oil.
An odour,
Warm diesel and Brylcream,
Clings to the cushions
On his favourite chair.
Fading tattoos
Meander up a mountain of muscle.
Bulging biceps,
Encrusted with grime,
Form a fleshy pier
In a harbour of hugs.

Norah Nelson

FFION SIONED

Eyes as dark as chocolate drops.
Hair as smooth and soft as silk.
A nature oh, so loving, and teeth
As white as milk.

This lady really is a beauty
Who has cute and winsome ways.
As she has such lavish parties,
When she celebrates her birthday.

On times she can be quite haughty,
With her head and nose held high in the air.
Especially to the opposite sex, or when her
Body language says, 'approach me if you dare.'

She dines very often upon chicken and pasta,
And chocolate drops are her favourite treat.
She visits the beauty parlour very often,
At last every six to eight weeks.

She will take a walk around the village
With a most regal air,
People will sometimes stop and chat to her,
Others can only stand and stare.

Are we speaking about royalty here, or maybe a movie star?
Oh no, no, no, surprise, surprise,
She is a loveable King Charles Cavalier spaniel,
Whose pedigree will go far.

Jean Evans

AUTUMN ANGEL

Summer begins to fade away.
Under the darkened sky,
Days are shorter, coats are worn,
On the weather you cannot rely.
A wrinkled face frowns and cries,
A tear trickles down its face,
Walking away from the ripe green trees,
Attempting to shorten its pace.
Now all I see is a limping friend,
Trudging through truth by my side,
Keeping the secrets of sunlight and joy,
Until the next year it will hide.
Keeping so quiet, nothing is said,
Painting the sky with its sorrow,
Dipping its brush into murky-grey streams,
To create the dim scene for tomorrow.
It limits enjoyment and sets the rules,
Of which nobody can break,
Strict and stubborn, it will not give in,
Ignoring the pleas you will make.
Breathing loudly, howls and groans,
Keeps you awake at night,
Where is the brightness once we owned?
It was lost in a natural fight.
Triumphant and proud, browns the fields,
An ink-pen is poised in its hand,
Writing the script of the homes' order,
Determines the state of our land.

Hayley Slade

MOVING ON

Will I remember
The weightlessness
And softness of a feather in my hand?
The many shades of green
In the countryside,
Bluebells shaking their heads
Bowing to
The brilliance of the sun,
A smile and the warmth it creates,
The swishing sound of waves,
Grating over pebbles and sand,
At one with nature,
Relaxing sense of peace flows by.

C R Coupe

PETITE FLEUR

(Inspired by Iris Hall)

Dainty and demure with a bygone grace,
No furrowed frown upon that sweet face,
That masks an iron will, a backbone of steel,
She takes life's knocks in her stride,
Disappointment she can hide.
As she greets you with a charming smile,
With twinkling eyes that beguile,
Who is this woman that inspires such poetic fame?
Iris is her name.

Anita Hopes

WITH ALL MY WISDOM

I woke up this morning to find
An envelope on the mat at the door,
There it sat, until I picked it up and tore it open,
To find the results staring back at me.
For sure I was expecting them some time soon,
But, it was still a shock to the system.
Listen up, I said to my friends,
'Hung-over' in my living room
From the party, the night before.
Whom was it that said,
With all my infinite wisdom,
I would never pass the test,
To be an envelope stuffer!
Well, I didn't, oh bugger.
Now I shall have to keep on knocking
On those opportunity doors.

Dillwyn Jones

LONELY PEOPLE

Only the lonely can sit and stir
All alone in their rocking chair
Looking at stars in the night or trees
In the day hoping the loneliness
Would go away
Some may like it some may not
It's all they have and all they have got
They know there are people
If they want to talk
They know there are roads
If they want to walk
Only the lonely can sit and stare
All alone in their rocking chair.

R Greaves

FIRST BIRTHDAY

We can't believe a year has flown
Since you arrived to make our lives.

Intriguing boy of active traits
Unceasing in your busy ways.

A daily clock within your head
Determines roughly what you do.

You eat and drink and crawl and play
And bodily adjust your life.

Adapting to the rushing days
An infant stoic in a whirling world.

Your laughing smiling earnest face
Is never still apart from sleep.

You're sunshine on each rainy day
A rainbow's end within our grasp.

Crawling, standing, climbing, walking . . .
All within a space of weeks . . . and

Soon will come the staggered run
As life unfolds before our eyes.

A twelve month evolution blitz
Of you and us and pride and love.

D B Kennedy

ONE MORE STAR

She knew the angels were coming that night,
Each time she looked up they had crept closer.
I could see it in her eyes,
The eyes which assured me,
Persuaded that this was the best way.
And there was a new star that night,
In the midnight blue of darkness.
Small.
New.
Yet to develop.
But there
And burning brightly with a special vigour,
Which said,
Now there is no more pain,
Now I am peaceful
And can be at rest.

Stephanie Hague

A Poem For My Mum's 58th Birthday

You were born in 1942 which makes you 58,
Your retirement garden awaits you standing at the gate
I can picture you now sat outside sipping afternoon tea
Rolling up your trousers and paddling in the sea,
You will have a caravan at the coast, visit when you can,
You will buy strawberries, plums, apricots and make loads of jam.
Everything you cook will involve using mince,
You will have curlers in your hair and scary purple rinse.
You will join a derby and Joan a club for the occasional dance,
You will have to wear rubber knickers, cos you will always
                                          pee your pants.
You won't remember names, you will just get all flustered.
You won't eat roast beef cos you'll have false teeth
And they would end up in your custard.
But you don't care whatever happens in those ageing years to come
You might be old and grey and senile but you'll always be my mum.

A Wright

GOING TO PIECES

My head is thumping,
Every bone in my body aches.
A searing pain has gone through my heart
And my spirit has fragmented into pieces.
Tears blur my eyes and constantly flow,
My beliefs ripped into shreds and
My soul torn completely in two.
Darkness descends and I pray for sleep
Please a brief respite from
My torturous thoughts.
Love, anger, sadness and grief
Flow through my veins and give me no peace.
Battered and bruised I drift into the haze,
Real sleep eludes me, no running from the pain.

Fredericka Durham

URGENT CONFUSION AND EVERYTHING WILL BE ALRIGHT

I need to get away from me,
I need to escape myself.
I need to take a break from me
And leave myself behind.

I need to get a grip on me,
I need to find control.
I need to take a look at me,
And learn that I can't hide.

I need to get away from you,
And leave you well behind.
I need to get a grip on me,
Cure myself inside.

F D Gunn

IT

Will anybody just stop and listen
Or am I a lifer in this prison?
Never a minute to give me their time
Shut up, or I will have committed a crime
Days turn to weeks with no time for a rest
Running around, bowing to their requests
The fact that I work all the hours in a day
And night for that matter, should be grateful for my pay
Insides turn outside, emotions can't handle
Shame I'm not 'in', their positions to wangle
Use and abuse with no thanks or respect
Cover their backs then become a reject
They say I'm not needed, they haven't a clue
About the difference between a football strip or tutu
26 members could cause confusion
But I'm now not required is the manager's conclusion
The smugness they feel when I'm knocked out of place
My standing demoted, fallen from grace
Where has my pride gone? They buckle me under
Cowering, afraid I'll make a blunder
Full of importance they like to gloat,
'You'll be out of here if you rock the boat'
A chicken, that's what I am
Terrified to voice the scam
But they'd gag me and bind me and show me the door
After 24 years my career's no more
I really can't help it, I feel like sh*t
Everyone's someone and I'm just an *'it'*

Kal Elias

Sunday Lovin' . . .

Ride with me on a summer's day,
to a shady copse where we will lay,
take my clothes off to my skinny,
I'll lick my last Rolo from your 'inny',
stroke my hair, kiss my face,
and feel the goosebumps as we embrace.
Skin on skin, closer than before,
making me want more, more, more!
Nuzzly nose against your neck,
one hundred velvet kisses down your back,
as we lay looking up at the trees,
the dappled sun shines through the leaves,
stop the clock, forget the time,
today I'm selfish, today you're mine!
So there I am, naked to see,
or is this just your fantasy?

Sarah Green

UNTITLED

You're so far away
Each centimetre a million miles
And through the space
I watch you
My mind embracing you
Feeling every contour
With my eyes
The touch of my fingers
Are your lips
The warmth of my pillow
Your arms
Your hand
Is the banister
That leads me to my room

Susan Hutchins

WHAT YOU ARE

You are the rose
In the garden,
You are the green
In the grass,
You are the sunlight
Of my life,
That's what you are.

You are the moon
Of my night,
You are the breeze
In the trees,
You are the bird,
Flying in the sky,
That's what you are.

You are the fish
In the sea,
You are my honey
From the bees,
You are the spring
Of my life,
That's what you are.

Nigel Moore

THE OLD OAK TREE

In the middle of the lawn
Sits the old oak tree
Older than the gardens
Older than the Grange
The branches reach down
Offering a place to rest
Birds build their nests
Fledglings take first flights
Squirrels scamper up the trunk
To stash away some nuts
Children climb and swing
Calling to each other
Parents sit beneath
Shaded from the sun
This tree has tales to tell
Of times gone by
Parties at the Grange
Carriages driving by
The Prince and his mistress
As they dally here
Nobility and merchants
Gentlemen and ladies
Riding on the downs
Sneaking a kiss
Hiding in the branches
A haven over time.

Maureen Ashing

BREAKING DOWN THE BARRIERS

You walked into my life and took me by surprise
Just when I was so proud of myself for being so strong
I was becoming used to a life
Without the enveloping warmth and closeness of another human being -
And now, you have thrown me completely -
You have made an assault on my emotions.
Simply from the look in your eyes
And the very depth of your understanding.
My heart says, 'I love you!'
But my mouth cannot say the words.

Ann Kemal

ELDERLY TODAY

One day I awoke,
caught a glimpse,
age-old haggard face,
fifty spoke my eyes.
Remember my supple body,
perked and alert, at nineteen,
how the years had passed so quick,
exchanging my once youthful looks
for knowledge I have gained.

On that day I awoke,
so much I recollect,
searching for answers in every new bright day.
How many did I find towards the end,
and now how I look,
what have I truly gained?
Basking in youthful games,
the ones we used to play,
the memories like photographs,
forever in my head.
Fifty passes and ninety resides,
upon my wrinkled face,
in every line there appears the loss of
one more youthful day.
It is a natural process,
but I never gave much thought
to being elderly today.
What I have truly gained
are those lifetime memories
where I still play.

Ryan T McManus

TO BE TRULY BLESSED

The sound of the ocean
The smell of a newborn
The view of a sunset
The touch of a loved one

The sound of my nephew laughing
The smell of my favourite meal
The view of my family enjoying themselves
The touch of a loved one

The sound of 'Happy Birthday'
The smell of a particular object that takes me back to childhood
The view of a book
The touch of a loved one

If I keep hold of all these things then I will be truly blessed.

Anthony R Neverson

ODE TO A TEA BAG

What do you do with your tea bag
When you've taken it out of the pot?
It's all wet and sloppy,
Droopy and soppy,
Squeezed and misshapen and hot.
Do you pit it to drain on your drainer
Or throw it in some dirty bin?
Or maybe it's tossed
On a smelly compost,
The way that it's treated, it's a sin.

Before you go using that tea bag,
You eye it with pride and delight,
Your aim is to savour
Its full-bodied flavour,
Whether by day or by night.
But as soon as you've scalded that tea bag,
It's ferociously stirred then thrown out.
Metaphorically speaking
Its end you are seeking,
Its destiny's right up the spout!

M Bulmer

ELUSIVE

Elusive as quicksilver
A candle in the wind
A mirage in the desert
A song some never sing
When you think you've
Grasped it in your hand
Like a thief it steals away
And the emptiness that's
Left behind
Will never go away

All fall beneath
The spell it weaves
Weak or strong
No one is free
When given you soar
On eagles' wings
Withheld you're on your knees
Yes love is such a fragile gift
Often lent but seldom owned
And broken hearts
And unshed tears
Is the interest on the loan.

A Fox

BEYOND THE NIGHT SKY

The night to me is endless,
through it I see tomorrow.
The future, that which is not yet true.
In the stars I see your eyes,
the sparkle of a memory,
the twinkle of a vision,
the shimmer of a thought.
The mists of the galaxies
hide the true lights.
Cloud your face and mine.
These are the waterfalls of life,
a cascading flow of lights.
On each one a different vision, thought or dream.
I see me up there.
Do I see me?
The stars burn out and after a while all that is left is the sun.

Amy Feather

CARING

There's some that care
And some that don't
There's some that think they do
A few who try to show they care
And some who do it's true

We try to show our feelings
In oh so many ways
We let our sharing, caring, show
In lots and lots of ways

To care for other people
Today is very rare
Times have changed about us
Of this we are aware

Why is it this has happened?
Why is it this way now?
Why can't we be a human race
Made up of those who care?

Sylvia Butcher

AN IDEAL WORLD

In an ideal world there's no colour, there's no creed,
There's no selfishness, no poverty, no greed.
Man's inhumanity to man is just a story, just a myth,
There are never wars or bombings, or mass deaths.
In an ideal world there is sunshine, rain and flowers,
Never fighting battles for the share of power.
Man would never destroy the dreams of every girl and boy
To grow up in a world of eternal peace.
But this world is just a dream to blot out the awful screams
Of a world that is dying from Man's hand.
He is intent on carrying out mass extermination,
Everything that's decent must be seen to be destroyed.
From pollution in the sea, to pollution in the air,
To pollution on the land and pollution to the Man.
No one cares it seems, why should they? There will always be
Another day to right all the wrongs and drop all the bombs
To make sure that everyone is subdued.
We are just helpless puppets of the masters
Oblivious to the need of simply living.
When it is too late to recall or relate or to discover
What life was like when people loved each other,
I wonder what the politicians will make as an excuse
That mankind is just another source of refuse.
I pray that on that day I am far away in another ideal world,
Where the value of each other makes us all just equal brothers
Under a canopy of undying love and peace.

Veronica E Terry

CRIME UNLIMITED

Whatever is happening in this country today?
There is crime on the streets everywhere,
People are robbed, pensioners mugged,
There are no police anywhere.
Many teenagers wander the streets,
They say they have nothing to do,
Yet there are many who go out to work,
But there are those who don't want to.
They need money so they rob and steal,
Many have drugs to buy,
Taking from others means nothing to them,
As long as they can get 'high'.
Years ago when I was a child,
Police always walked the streets,
No police cars in those days,
They did the job on their feet.
They always had time for everyone,
With a kind word and a smile,
Wherever, whenever, they earned respect,
Their job was always worthwhile.

M James

WINTER

I'm just like the withered woods
At the roadside wasting away
And languid like the litter in the lane.

I've come to the margin of the meadow
And look back at what's gone before
But I reside recumbent and won't roam no more
And dwell in my cabin in the glen.

The cold snap of winter wind
Will call us once again
And all my feathered friends
Will gather in the trees outside my door
Then away go once more to pastures new
And share with me in the sorrow of my woe.

The memories of my early days
Bring the magic of my former years
When I was a lusty lad and dreamt of times long ago
I dreamt of days gone by and never roam again
The final chapter is etched in stone
But never heard again.

James T Dennison

POP A PILL

Feeling low I hear you say
'Pop a pill, things will be OK
Make you feel better.'
I can do that,
Just take a pill,
Never think about the fact
That you might need another
To follow after that.

Jenny Wylie

FRIENDSHIP

What a wonderful gift it is, friendship,
To find it is very rare.
Young or old to find all the wonders
Of caring and trusting that it can give.
So look to friendship
With the greatest care
And thank God for giving you
This wonderful friendship.

J Clothier

ALZHEIMER'S JOURNEY

No one said 'twould be easy;
But that's the price that some pay.
Our path has been cut out before us,
By a generation of yesterday.

So what is the cost that we owe them?
Can gratitude be measured in gold?
They ask for nothing -
For life meant just duty.

Remember that when they are old.

Windsor Hopkins

OH HAPPY, GLORIOUS MAY

May is the month full of hope and promise,
After the cold chill of winter!
Slowly the first flowers of spring appear,
Snowdrops so pretty and white,
Tulips and daffodils dancing in the breeze!
Yes! May is indeed a month to be glad,
With its promise of new life
And flowers that say, 'Take heart!'
See, here we are again, now the winter is past,
Like the Easter message, we say, 'Take heart!'
See, we have risen again, as one day you shall!

Angela M Denton

BEAUTIFUL ROSE

Rose,
Sweet rose,
Smelling so sweet,
Making me high,
Beautiful rose
And with your short, sharp thorns,
You tear and shred,
Pain erupts,
But beauty covers,
Your sharpness lost,
As beauty smothers
Such pain,
Such agony,
But so much beauty.

Emma Mitchell

A LONG AWAITED VISIT

I didn't visit you for ages,
Today was the first time in a long while,
You both looked sick, with the cold,
Waiting for a bowl of warm soup.
He kept filling the fire with coal,
She sat and smoked, and watched on,
And I sat bemused at the sight in front of me,
As long as they have each other, they are happy.
They look old, but in their eyes contentment appears,
He coughs so loud, he mumbles as he speaks,
She turns down the TV because she can't hear him.
He gets up and goes into the garden,
Filling up bread packages with slack.
He feeds the neighbourhood stray cats,
And then they run to the next house.
I sit and listen as they tell me of old times,
I felt a deep sadness that I never visited them sooner,
But I'm glad I visited them today.

Dee Hawkins

BAR ROOM SHUFFLE

There's a smoke-filled bar down the back street
White lights, fog lights, glow behind the bar
An old man sits and takes another whisky
No hope, poor soul, he's gone too far

There's a cold wind blowing at the doorway
The smoky heat blows warm into the street
A young body standing in the portway
Shoes clicking to a high-heeled beat

Black skirt and coat and handbag
Black stockings tight from thigh to feet
Black hair sweeps bold across her shoulder
Body oozing body heat

Fresh in for the night-time's drinking
Filter tip stuck in hot-red lips
Sipping iced gin and tonic water
Waiting for you to nudge her hip

It's a hot night down in the bar room
As they call for the last drinks of the day
She smiles and says, 'Hey there, Johnnie,
Time you and me were on our way.'

John M Winters

CHANGE

As seasons change and May begins,
From spring to summer, this month brings
Flowers so bright, colours so gay
That bring us into the month of May.

A burning ember, a spark, a light,
To guide my way - to a future bright.
From beyond times past, so full of despair
To faith and hope this time of year.

This is the month, I see so clear,
A joyous occasion, a wish so dear
To walk down the road and carry no fear.
A burning desire to achieve my goal
To find my way, I keep it in the day,
This is the wisdom of the month of May.

Peter Cranswick

NAPSBURY

There it stands a shadow of its former glory,
disintegrated through time's careless ruin.
Oblivious to its pre-eminent demise,
its architecture echoes of an era long since gone.
As former patients strive to comprehend the outside world,
it in turn neglects them.
An institute that was once their home,
now heartlessly deserts them.

John Warren

AMIDST THE FELLS

Walking in the mountains
ponder there is no better place to be.
Stepping through Wordsworth's daffodils -
They bow their heads as I pass.
Wondering, lonely as I pass a hidden tarn.
As I rest do I spy
in the corners of my mind -
as I imagine Coleridge, Southey, Wordsworth and De Quincey
on my walk and long climb.
I reach the snow-covered cairn,
to find the cross winds are strong,
blowing me bitterly and I'm blindingly cold.
While the mist is obscuring for
Rydal and Thirlmere I cannot see.
As Grasmere and its village are somewhere beneath me.
Does anybody know I am up here?
While the Lion and the Lamb
I use as a wind-breaker,
but I'm sure they won't tell!
A good shot of whisky
warms the cockles of my heart,
as my fingers and nose
are feeling numb from the cold.
Now I have eaten and rested my weary bones,
the time is getting on
as I get up to descend.
Hoping to arrive back in Keswick
before nightfall.

Anthony Clarke

FAITH

To believe in yourself,
to truly believe who you are.
To have commitment to learn,
to find knowledge and understanding.

To trust the way you feel,
to be sure of the right feeling.
To be steadfast and strong,
to face mockery and insult.

To breathe clean air,
to be able to laugh out loud.
To love unconditionally,
to listen without prejudice.

To truly believe,
is to live life with faith.

Karen Margaret Barnes

UNITY

Looking out the dirty old window wondering why the world is moving so slow? People in a hurry with nowhere to go, I'm confused and it shows, I'm in a world of my own, like so many others I'm all alone, why are we all alone? In front of me are so many roads and I'm unsure of which way to go.

People wake up, get up and set your goals, I'll help you if you're alone. We'll make new rules and conquer all the roads with two of us we'll become strong. When we're three it'll become unity, not forgetting it's another mouth to feed, but don't you see we're now a family and that's unity.

Unity that's the key
I say black is beautiful
you say white is right
I say put them together to make this world right
UNITY that's unity

Rains started falling, our lips are not moving, why are we not talking, is it because raindrops are rolling? It's a mystery to me, why is it you cannot see how much you mean to me and it will always be the three of us in unity. I want the world to see how much you mean to me.

Unity, that's the key.

Eugene Dunkley

MOMENTS IN TIME

I feel so at ease with this man,
We talk together as only we can.
I long one day for his body to touch,
The desire I feel moves me so much.
His eyes are friendly in every way,
Each day I see him is a bonus day,
The joy I feel in my heart,
Will always be; how did it start?
I feel he does not, cannot know,
How I feel, so high, so low.
The friendliness in his face
Makes my very pulses race.
Will always feel at one with him,
Even when my eyes grow dim.
I'm so happy when he talks to me,
It's my only joy, I can see.
I hope the day never comes my way
When I'll not see him day by day,
I would feel so very sad,
And wish for times we could have had.

Olive Young

UNTITLED

Like a small poisonous snake
Lying under a devilish curse,
Warning of danger,
Ready to punish severely.
Be careful of the force and power,
It will deceive,
With a violent attack,
It will cause pain.
'But do not worry,' I say.
'Let me be calm,
And let my courage in times of trouble
Put to death these evils.'
This I will command,
For I am good!

Darren Kimberley

UNTITLED

I will go to my bingo today
I will enjoy my play.
I might even get a shout,
That will make a great day out.
Even if I don't shout
I will enjoy my day out.
The people that go to the bingo
Are a friendly crowd.
They talk to one another
That's what it's all about.

Cecilia Forbes

FEELINGS

A   is for anger like a volcano erupting.
B   is for boredom, watching rain trickle down the window.
C   is for courage to try something new,
D   is for determination to reach the highest mountain.
E   is for eagerness, like a spaniel waiting for a biscuit.
F   is for fear, feeling uncomfortable and terrified.
G   is for gloomy, feeling down and depressed.
H   is for happiness, watching a baby take its first steps.
I   is for insecure, feeling unsafe and worried.
J   is for joy, feeling bouncy and fantastic.
K   is for kindness, being genuine and caring.
L   is for loneliness, feeling down and unhappy.

Rachel Louise Ashton (10)

EMERALD ISLE

The snort of the burro
disturbed by fleas
in the early dawn light.

Fragrant smells of peat fires.
Hedgerows heavy with
May splendour.

To tramp alone through
deserted fells,
catch sight of Croix Patrick

looming through the mist,
scaled by hordes of sinners
praying for redemption.

Many varied greens evoke
primeval longings
to be near my forefathers

in my beautiful
Emerald Isle.

Margaret Robers

REFLECTIONS ON HUMANITY

'What a tangled web we weave when we practice to deceive . . .'
No quotation half as true, I wonder now could it mean you?
So much cruelty Man bestows, without a mark for it to show;
So much harm by word, by deed, tell me truly is there need
To hurt another soul like this? Indeed for some it seems it's bliss.
What nasty natures some possess, it's true they could not live with less.
From spiteful tongues without a measure, it seems to give them so
much pleasure.
To twist another's word for gain and cause that other person pain.
The world can be a wicked place, no matter creed, no matter race.
Abuse of children now is rife, without a qualm for taking life.
Beatings, killings all abound, there seems so much of it around.
Appears to be so full of crime, is this the fashion of our time?
So much jealousy and hate, surely this can't be our fate.
For I have seen another side, a side I'm sure has not yet died.
Where down a leafy lane you'd tread, without a thought of any dread.
To see a field of waving corn, upon a lovely summer's morn
And hear the birds sing in the trees, the sound of softly humming bees.
Animals left free and well and in their rightful place to dwell.
People smiled and said hello, and in their hearts they meant it so.
I've seen a child smile trustingly, when she looked up so sweet at me.
We helped another if we could, most people wanted to do good.
For God above made us as one, He'd made no barriers when He'd done.
He gave us brains to show our worth, to see what we could do on Earth,
And when it's time to take our rest, can we tell Him we've done
our best?

E M Housman

ECLIPSE ON AT THE THEATRE

Eclipse is on at the theatre
With the sun and moon taking the main role
Nature in the supporting cast,
The stage a vast expanse
All the audience looking like ants,
Clouds opening and closing for curtains
But far more dramatic and startling,
At the main part of the play
The moon, blots the sun's rays,
Causing darkness to descend on Earth.

To all life it is so awesome
Then the moon slips slowly off stage,
As the sun is back for the last act,
Such splendour, she is wearing a diamond ring,
And like a thousand flashlights dazzling,
There is thunderous applause,
Too many curtain calls.

Susan Archer

FIGHTING THE NIGHT

It's now closing time at the 'Olde Tea Shop'
and willowy, crunched silhouettes stoop out
into the dying afternoon embers.
At once, they're engulfed, cast away,
unrecognisable to each other
in the surge of promenade passers-by.

Only then, they drift, the impetus gone
beneath a fluttering line of lights
which shine beacon-like in willing pockets
and punch holes in the irresistible dusk.

This is where the action is, a few feet up,
fighting the onset of darkness, between
two posts; a stubborn chain of rebellion.

Over the railings, sort of all at sea,
a lone figure kicks through the remains of
kids' castles or fathers' fortresses.
He too wonders when the tide will turn.

No matter. The boys have rounded the corner,
riotously wheeling their way somewhere.
They catch up with the frail fraternity,
then leave those behind who were once young.

This is where the action is, not amongst
the swathes of sand with a beachcomber
who needs the sea to whisper him answers.

It lies in these lads fighting the night.
It lies in us all seizing the day
and it lies up there where the clutch of
lights snap restlessly at the morbid sky.

Ian Corns

DID YOU NOT KNOW?

When I look deep
into your silent brown eyes
I see the eternal light
of all the moons
of all the suns
that have shone down through
the dark ages of man.

I see all the scars,
the wars, the pain, the joy,
the fears, the love
of everyman.

Did you not know the universe is in your eyes?
Did you not know that life is in your lips?

Did you not know that the truth is in your words?
And that the way to Heaven is through your heart?

Michael J Davies

PERHAPS

Perhaps - possibly - maybe
Making decisions are hard to see
With all the options
That appear to be.
This one - that one
Which will it be?

Questions to ask
Answers to be found
Never as easy as it sounds.
Why the doubt that fills your mind
When a 'yes' or 'no'
Is what you will find.

Perhaps - possibly - maybe
Again and again, over and over,
A quandary. It seems
To be never ending.
Till someone else steps in
To make the decisions for me.

Dorothy Boulton

AMELIA

When I look at you, Amelia,
I sigh.
When I think of you, Amelia,
My heart goes a thumpin'
I'm not sure why -
Please say 'yes' to my request, Amelia,
Cos I'm Tim (no not dim!) -
That likeable guy.

B Montague

UNTITLED

Tears drip from my spirit,
a dehydrated shell is all that's left,
cold, empty, confused, hollow pool,
quench my thirst,
life shadowed by death.

Danny Gilites

How To Write A Poem

Anyone can write a poem,
Just pick up a pen and get going,
You don't even need a good subject,
Pick out words just like insect,
But the confusing thing in this poetry,
Is how the lines lay, 6, 5, 4 or 3,
Do I need to write my first line like this,
And then have one that follows,
Or should I have a 3rd line, Miss?
But the structure then is hollow,
But hollow is a hatfull or so the saying goes,
So if we're saying sayings then it isn't so.

Now if you want to write for fun,
Then let your pen just run and run,
Express yourself, don't be embarrassed,
Any words will do we don't care less,
Shakespeare, Burns, Keats all had their ways,
But would they have held up these days,
With racism, prejudice and political correctness?
Their poems would have been quashed before
They were witnessed.

My message here is loud and clear,
Write for fun without any fear,
Of upsetting people whoever they are,
Family or friends near or far,
A poem is as easy as you want,
So all you bards can come and haunt,
All the classrooms across the nation,
Because our next poets are the next generation.

Sam Cooper

HOPE

When you look about you
What do you see?
The sun, the moon, the sky,
Or can you hear the sea?

As you walk along
With your shirt tail hanging out,
Do you feel that there's
No one about?

It's a strange old world we live in,
Where no one really cares,
If you go about your business,
Or fall down the stairs.

But in saying all of this,
I do believe there's hope,
Maybe some day
We will be blessed
By the Pope!

G Barrett

THE WORKER

Lived in Acton north of Wapping
Worked from five to sixty-five
Rose at six from an early bed
To go and earn his daily bread
Lived through a war that claimed his wife
Now all he has are souvenirs
One gold watch from Jones and Son
Six old medals from World War One
And when it's time for him to go
And all the gifts of life go out
Is this what life is all about?

Roy Hilleard

ALL OF A SUDDEN IT HAPPENED

It happened oh so suddenly
I didn't think it real
I seemed to live for days and days
In just a lovely dream
I walked on air
I couldn't eat
Feet so tired but couldn't sleep
I didn't know just what it was
And then we speak
The dream now seems so very real
The reason is so simple
We are in love, you and I
So ever more I'm thinking,
It always happens suddenly
But couldn't quite imagine,
Someone like 'you' could love me
So forever more I'm sinking, into a daze,
Each time I see, you standing there, waiting.

Georgette Marina Poole

A SAINT VALENTINE'S DAY COCKTAIL

Some secret this
When I who write
Must surely give away,
With much delight,
The answer, 'Me',
To your question, 'Who'?

If I liken you
To calm green days
And mellow sun,
Buttressed by rocky coasts
And curling seas,
You'll find the natural closeness
Of land and sea -
Of you and me.

If I liken you
To cooling nights of coloured lights,
'Neath velvet skies,
With stars twinkling low,
Let music with laughter
And crystal, ice cold, tinkling,
Fold the night away,
To dawn as Saint Valentine's Day.

Brian Christopher Wilkinson

PETS

When we feel unhappy our pets make us feel better
Because on good days and bad days
They are always there for us.
They are our best friends
In every hour of every day
We love our pets more than life itself
For life would be very empty
If there were no pets.

Oliver Carlin

SILENCE

Silence, silence all around,
Except for the rhythmic ticking of the clock,
Pounding our lives away; so systematic,
The second-hand, as though racing with its inner self,
Taunting us with each revolution it attains,
The speed with which each cycle is attained is incredible.

Time makes its steady progression,
The second hand in full swing,
The hand does not smoothly run,
It jerks each second for us to see.
But what is a second? A second could be nothing to recall
Or a second could be eternity after all.

B Turner

CLOAKING THE SIGH OF BURNT FORESTS

Long since past the scaffolds' cold discipline
Softly stroking her father's pre-death blames
Each darkness a glass blurs that splutter
Faint as ash on concrete before it croaked
Empty smiles it's always been
Nothing, senseless nature recycling
A vision made of snuffwire words
His crooked wood spine controls till the line
A replacement drunk cradling a clean baby
Beating the redundant tears from her cheek
Happy home of colostomy

Andrew Gibson

COGS OF THE NIGHT CITY

I enter you: a cold machine.
Myself and countless others mirror
faceless grey pigeons entering you also,
oiling your intolerable cogs.

Miles underground, we worm through your passages:
filthy-faced miners fuelling a hidden furnace.
While above, your street-veins are afire with surging energy.
Intoxicating lights beckon moths onto the flame.
Rogue city. Relentless night-plough: we satisfy ourselves
on the small morsels that you church up in your wake.
We all man our stations. The monsoon continues.
Un-harboured, I stand alone and wait until morning.

Dan Blake

WORDS

I knew that I could do it
it was just a matter of when,
to tickle all these little words
and make them jump out of this pen.

They landed on this paper
and just fell right into line,
what clever little words they are
telling stories just like mine.

They make us happy, mostly
depending on what's been wrote,
but how many times have they made you cry
and brought a lump into your throat?

Words don't know any different
'cause it's the hand that wields the pen,
if you find the pen's not in the mood
use a pencil, now and then (ha ha).

You've got to hand it to poetry
Words express things oh so nice,
None of them have to rhyme either
So I can end this line with anything, see!

What a fantastic way to communicate
for the pen is mightier than the sword,
whatever would this world be like
without a single, beautiful word?
God bless 'em, and keep writing!

Chris Thomas

SIDES OF A COIN

One side of the coin

Is a child
Lost in the wilderness
Sobbing, unloved
No family
No friend
No one who cares.

The other

Is the crazy monster
Who seeks revenge
Upon all those
Who beat it
Into the desert
Of despair.

And yet another

I wish to be neither
Yet I am both
They are me
We must make peace
Move on, let go
Be free.

Trevor De Luca

YOUR BEAUTY, MY DEAR

Fountains are beautiful
Waterfalls and trees
But all are gracefully brought
To their knees
By your beauty, my darling,
That shines so bright,
That shines like
The beautiful stars in the night.
How do you shine so bright
Making other stars disappear?
I know the key to you
The key to your heart, my dear . . .
When God began to make you
He asked you for one wish.
He asked you what you wanted
To live a life of bliss,
You asked Him in a humble voice,
'Well, God, there is one thing
I would like to look as good
On the outside only as I am on the in.'
And so it shows God granted your wish -
So beautiful in and out
So humble, kind and generous
With beauty no man could doubt.

Nicky Hooper

A MOMENT IN THE STORM

Is it morning or is it evening?
The grey clouds my judgement,
Stillness, calm anticipation;
The winds hold their breath.
I walk along the road, alone,
Unafraid, embracing the darkness,
And then, without a warning it begins.
Droplets burst from their gloomy prison,
Falling to Earth, tasting freedom,
Nothing can stop them,
For they are invincible, immortal.
I turn my head to the spouting skies,
Rain cascades down my face,
Soaking everything in its unknown path.
The air is filled with magical static,
A jagged shard of light breaks the spell,
Angry thunder beats through the streets.
I will not run for cover, I will not hide,
As the storm beats only for me.

Karen Johnson

DAY TRIPPER

Her bikini is scant
You say. The poser.
Her toned, tanned body.
Her tiny waist and big extremities.
I envy her gall.

From your gaze. Your cool gaze.
I snap her on camera
We bask in the sunshine
Like page three. Pouting lips.

Unglued eyelashes - wilt in the heat.
The girl who can't keep her pose.
She topples. The natives observe
And grin.

Bedraggled you emerge from the depths.
Your kiss is salty. Our day trip to
The island is a wash out.
Beauty is its own reward.

Dawn Sansum

THE NIGHT IS DARK

The night is dark and the rains are incessant.
The trees in the garden are swaying to and fro
like wailing women.
The mourning wind like a fugitive forlorn groans
in the wilderness.
The starless sky deluges the world with tears.
The lightning with a sudden flash lays bare the
world's weeping heard.

Lo the sublime has arisen to judge the world and
its wrongs.

My heart trembles and throbs in His presence to
find myself utterly lonely and insignificant before
His magnificence.

From a distant hut there comes the vague notes of
a restless flute player and my heart dances with
joy and relish to find that I am not alone before
the sublime:
The unknown flute player is also with me
united we shall suffer the worst at His hands with
songs on our lips.

J K Desai